Dedicated to:

People who didn't read the first book

Table of Contents

Awww Poems 1

Oh… Poems 122

Awww Poems

I Drink Glass

I prefer to drink champagne from a coffee mug
than to drink water from a wine glass

Pennies Are Overrated

I throw soda-can tabs
And green apple stems
In the fountains
Instead of pennies
Pennies are for the children
On the graves
And the driver's seat
But tabs and stems
Are for wishes
That truly have potential
They aren't selfish
Or harmful
Nor full of greed
Or desire
Only sincerity

What About XES

CENSORED

I am horny all the time
Now before you get dirty with it let me explain
I'm horny for cuddles and coffee and good books
To be horny doesn't mean to be sexual. It is having a deep desire
when it's lacking in that moment. It is desperation mixed with
stimulating pleasure
Be horny for life

A Nutcracker Christmas Rehearsal
(That's When This Happened)

What could our future look like
A simple candle and spaghetti
A Jack and coke with red lighting
A dance floor with strobes
A snowy night with small talk
But all it would be
Was a quick comment
Heart beating rapid
Smile on my face
Quietly laughing out of
Accomplishment
And nothing after
Acquaintance
Yet you insert yourself into my dreams
Even after 2 years later

Suffocating on Turbulence

You got me feeling some sort of way
And it's not the turbulence
Or the butterflies I get from the shaky plane
You make my heart soar higher than it ever has
And that's why I can't breathe anymore

Charcoal Face Mask

Allow yourself to see others
In a crowd of selfish faces

Put Some Clothes On

aren't you tired of swimming through my mind?
let me give you a break so you can catch your breath
i'll go find your towel so you can dry off
from skinny dipping in my head
allow me to fluff the pillows in my atriums
since you seem to have made a home in my heart

Suntanning Under Oven Lights

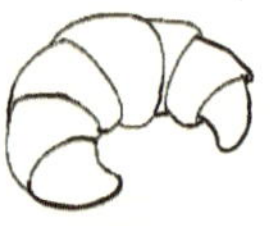

I bake in the wake of dusk
Each pastry glowing by the light of the oven
The shadows cast on the grey steel tray
Or a single spotlight
On main stage, up front and shining, blunt
And the bread which grows in luminescence
Reminded me more of the sun Rise

Your Eyes Feel Like Metal

For your eyes to make contact with the words I've written on
this page makes me feel like you're unlocking the words to my
soul

18

Well, That Was Intense

All I can hope is that
By the time our eyes
Are dug out by spoons
That our souls can
Float up at the same time
Because I honestly
Can't imagine "it"
Whether it be life or death
Without you.

Let's Buy A Magnifying Glass

I will be selfish, yet honest
I don't want anyone but you
I have barely met you
But I know I want you
And maybe I need you
Had we talked two years ago
Who knows what we're missing.
Or what is yet to come
It could be by December 8th
Or April 23rd
Who knows what could be.
Given one thing be different
Then it was

History Class Was Boring

Who is gonna tell your story
Who is gonna make you a legacy
Will it even matter, your transparency?
You'll be a ghost of no conspiracy
Just history passing on the writings of your ancestry
Forgotten by the ones who see
You were meant to be
Remembered
Perfectly.

My Feet Hurt

Something more
A moment longer
I haven't let you have a minute more
In my mind
But you alone
Spend hours
Tap dancing through my head
In my mind
My dreams
I still wonder
How?
I'm not complaining
But this must mean
It means something
Even to you
For me to be a familiar face
A Known.

Honey, Where's My Hammer?

Is decadence so wrong to have
To see that the society we live in
Can be rebuilt by us, our consciousness
For what we use to live in has passed
And the builders are dead
Is it so wrong to build a new future
In our image?
This is not the story of Narcissus
Repeated.
We know those mistakes
But build a society for our future generations
And their well-being
Is it so wrong to be presently "selfish" as so?

Use Your Last Braincell For This One

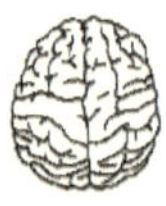

I long for the conditioned life of a loner
Not the determined life of a celebrity
To be a conditioned conditioner is to be free
To be the determined determiner is to be a dictator

I Stole Hermes' Shoes

I've run after so many of them
As cinematic as it sounds
I watch as they walk away
Step by step, they further the distance between
And I don't care if I must run a mile
I will run after *you*
To hug you
To hold you
To feel you in my embrace
And let you know you're safe in my arms
Even though I'm the one catching my breath
I will run after you
No matter the distance

I Fell Off A Seesaw Once

Why are you still on my mind
Your world on my axis
But you barely know me
I barely exist
It's way too uneven
It shouldn't make sense
That you're stuck in my head
And I'm stuck finding sense

Poetry Is Lunch

Reading diverse poetry is the gateway to a whole new spiritual culture. It is a means of feeding my spirit.

Wishing Upon a Speck of Glitter

The glitter on my eyelashes
Replay the shooting stars
Under the streetlight
And offer me
Countless
Wishes

Villanelle
(The Assassin From BBC)

If you shall sail away tomorrow, dear
May I pass by the foaming white beach side
And lay my soul to rest beneath the pier

How can I live if I live in this fear?
Not enough times, i tried, you tried, we tried
And soon you'll sail away tomorrow, dear

Is it worth living worlds away, from here?
Or worth living without your love, your bride?
If so, I'll lay my soul below the pier

My heart like an anchor, it pulls you near
But distance binds me underneath the tide
How can you sail away today, my dear?

May I sink to the ocean floor, so clear
The waves stroking my feet with every stride
And soon burry my soul beneath the pier

My heart is soaked and salty as a tear
All of my bones have somehow pruned inside
And now you are sailing away, my dear
I lay my soul to sleep beneath the pier

Who Needs Water Anymore?

Dare I call it love
You can be so infatuated
With someone you barely know
The hair and the eyes
Are first
And so nice.
And even when you're
Intoxicated they
Turn your world sober

So, How's the Navy?

I wear your bracelet every night
I cave into people
And wish you were here
You aren't manipulative
You're persuasive
In the best way
And that's why I wish you were still here

Anyone Seen My Keys?

Even if I'm dealing with my own thing
With my own car
At my own place
In my own house
On my own time
I'll be happy that I have something that's *mine*.

Saggie Pants

I am nobody to someone
But not nothing to anybody
And that's what makes me
A Sagittarius

O.nly L.etters M.atter

How pathetic is it
That I wait for stamps in the mail
- to save money -
Before sending your letter
For all I know
You could be hurt
Hurting
Gone.
One or two weeks
Makes a big difference
Now is the time

Now is all we have

So why wait?
I apologize
I apologize
But I know you'll love me
Always
Even if it's too late
Twin flame
Soul mate
Understanding
Whatever it is.
That's why I love you in a different way.

My Ear Is Bleeding

I miss your song
And it's not even your song
It's the one that reminds me of you
But one day you'll know.
I love you. So much ♡

Jobs Suck
(Get A Career)

If you liked essays in college, be a writer
If you want to do research in professionalism, be a writer
If you want to write musicals, be a writer
If you want to write every day, be a writer
If it's something you enjoy but don't get paid much for
Be a writer

I Got Dementia

Somehow, I've waited
A thousand years for you
Yet I don't know you
Who are "you"
Time can heal
But what is *time*
Without a body to inhabit time
I've waited
A thousand years
For, maybe not someone
But something.
A feeling.

Shut Up, George Bailey

What a beautiful life that we get to
Experience the feeling of being inebriated
Being bake and burned out
Being in love and giving love and receiving love
Oh what a lovely life

Tape My Eyes Open

Stay awake
No matter what
No matter who
No matter where
(Okay Michael Scott)
You look after them
Tuck them in
Keep them safe
You're alright
And you love
You.
(And them).

Black and White Films
(Are Not Racist)

As Collins describes the "ashen newsreels"
So I wish our love story
Could be a monochromatic movie
Manners and all
As the music swells our ears
To meet our cheek and nose and lip
For the perfect ballad
Strings softly in the moonlight

I Forgot Who This Was About

You're not attached to your body at all
Fumbling and falling all over the place
Yet your mind is in any place it can be
France, New York, Liverpool
Anywhere
There is something poetic about losing the feeling
Of being human
In one moment of numbness
Things feel as though it might be okay

You Taste Like Morgan

As crass as it sounds, it's impossible to be buzzed around you
No matter the amount I drink,
Just the thought of you
Sobers me up
Even after a hefty 50% alcoholic intake
You are my natural detox and that's what scares me the most
But that's what tells me it's true

Use Your Fingers
(Ew! Not Like That)

For the first to touch the fifth, comes the third
But the first to touch the fifth and the fourth births the second
And only the second can give you the ONE

68

I Was A Ghost Writer in College

BOO!

May you exist in literary jealousy
Enough to not paralyze you literarily
But instead literally
To not plant inspiration on you
But instead live in you

I'm Not Encouraging Cheating

You two are perfect
Will I find the person?
I refrain from saying "the one."
Why subject yourself to one person
Most people can be a mistake
But many are a blessing
I'm waiting for the person
To make things
A little better

Look It Up on WebMD

Wow, my giveaway is a shakiness
I'm an earthquake on a sunny San Francisco day
I can go from 3 to 8 in a second
PMD confuses my body
(Google it)
No matter the emotion
I shake at the strength of my feelings
It can be poetic yet destructive
Control doesn't truly exist
But that can be wonderful
In the right place

Become A Depressed Billionaire

All the money in the world won't make you happy
A gorgeous view will never satisfy you
Tear stained dollars rest in your wallet
Untouched, neglected
Bored.
They don't matter

But you.

I'm Forcing You to Do This

What's the best thing that's happened to you?
That's right.
I'm talking to YOU
Take a minute (a whole 60 seconds) and come back to me.
♡

♡

♡

I mean it. Think.
♡

♡

♡

Did you think about it? If you didn't, do it now. Last chance.
Close your eyes and think
-
Just know, whatever it is, that's what makes you lovely.
I mean it, I don't even know you.
But I love you for your desires and interests and passions.
I love you.
As a stranger or not, I love you
Believe it or not.
Thank you for thinking about something good in your life.
It makes me happy

Got Any Melatonin?

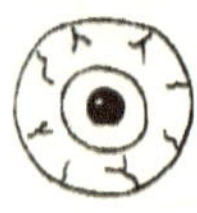

That's alright if not
But I'm even scared of the stars
And the floor
And looking up at you
- To you -
In your bed
Looking down at me

Narcissism sucks.
But sometimes you suck too.
(Still love you though)

(and myself......... I'm working on that)

I Don't Own A Parachute

I heard that song just yesterday
And want to make it my number one
Right now.
That's how you know I fall for things quickly
Even songs
Maybe that's better than people
Real people.
That's what keeps me "happy"
Optimistic?
Some word like that

Welcome to Commitment

It's our fault
That's an interesting thing to think about
Does this count as "relationship bonding?"
Talk?
Are we working it out?
Maybe it's okay if it's both our faults
Maybe that's why I always say
I'd rather die together
Than alone.

I'm Hanging Out with Alice
(Guess Where We Are)

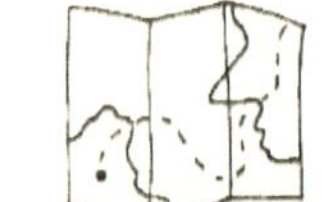

You want originality to the point where it's unique but still
hovers around the comfort zone of modern poetry – so why are
you and I lost

86

over here.

I Have A Crush On My Radio

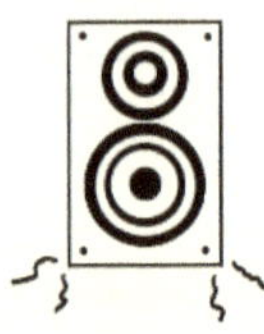

Having a crush is like
Hearing your favorite song
Without singing along
You hear it
You feel it
You groove to it
You simply react to it
But something is preventing you from singing along
Fear of judgement?
Opinion.
Taste.
Fear of too many things
Sing like you're alone
Blasting the bass through your car speakers –
The one time you "truly" get to be alone –
Sing like you're at a concert
The person next to you can't even hear you
Because even they are lost in
The Moment

How Cliché

No drug can make me feel the way you do
You *are* my drug
And that's the best high I could ever truly experience

Who Are You Again

Trust me, she will assume.
And as they say
"Expectations are planned disappointments."
At first, it was one poem
But second looks show there's more than five
So why wouldn't she think
There are poems for her in this book?
Maybe there are
But everyone will think
It's written for them

That's the beauty of poetry

Repetition.

Narcissists will think it's about them
Wanderers will wish it's about them

Green Fingers

You're as worn down as the ring you wear
What once had writing on it
Was scratched off by wood
Rough play
And aggressive bodies
But you never take it off
Because no matter how illegible
The writing is,
You keep wearing it
Because it is valuable to you
Even when it looks cheap
And broken to everyone else

I Hate the Dentist

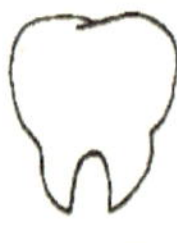

Even with a needle through my gums
I will squeeze your hand gently
As to not break your fragile bones
It doesn't matter the pain I go through
I won't allow you to feel
Any type of pain comparable to mine

Buddy Is My Go-To Name Now

I'm so sorry, Buddy.
You know who you are.
I left your letter on the desk.
But I know you're doing well
At least I hope
I'd rather be with you than you with me
Just know.
I'm proud of you.
I'm so proud of you.

Your Superpower Should Be Telepathy

It's okay.
At this point, I'm so talked out
And I wish my mind was
A loud separate being
Like dualism
But the mind is not separate from the body.
And you're stuck with your thoughts forever.
Aren't you glad no one else can
Hear your inner voice?
Cause I sure am

Theatre
(Not Theater.)

The moon is an understudy for the sun
As its light reflects off the glass
Making the scratches on the window
Play the part of comets
While the black sky
Is casted as a dark blue night with freckled stars

Drinking Drool

You can go forever
Pretending you don't value the words
That spill from your lover's mouth
Whether you can tell if it's a drip
Or an overflow
Anything from them will be
Some source of water
And water is necessary to live

Pinch Me

Is it wrong to dream
About you when you are
In the same room as I?
To believe it might come true
By a single manifestation
Or a stupid wish
I'm not sure what I believe,
But I
Shall be with you
Soon

Alcoholic Texting

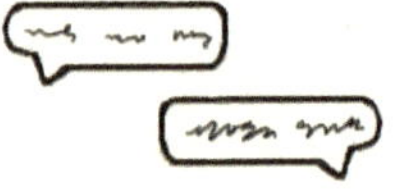

"But I hope you call me back
When you get too drunk
Yeah, I'm only being honest" - PB
Though it's entertaining to know
I'm the one calling you.
Maybe this song is about me
After all
Too weak, desperate, lonely.
Whether it's a friend or a lover,
Know that you're the one on my mind

Do You Lift Weights?

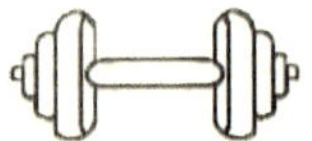

You're a lot stronger than I am
And that's an understatement
I don't have the right words
Cause you've broken yourself -
And my own heart that one night -
But every night it feels like I've experienced that pain
That PTSD
Yet it's nothing compared to yours
That's why I love you because
Damn, I don't know how you do it.

This Would've Been A Cheesy Song

I fell in love on a
Porch swing in Maine
It took some time
Till you called out my name
You came and sat down
Your seat next to mine
Our pinkies touched
And it slowed down my time
Nothing's felt this perfect in a while
Fairy tales I'm stuck in and I smile

Swing Dance
(Done the Wyoming Way)

Pretzels are nice for a moment
Cuddles stay for two more
But all you can hope
Is that bodies touch
During the dance
Every night
Wednesday
Thursday
But never Friday
Welcome to the bar.

I Can't Find the Last Piece
(And It's Pissing Me Off)

I watch myself in the reflection of the window
Each split end, each fly-away
Yet when I look at my face
My face.
I see you.
You've become a part of me
That's how far we've come, so far
So far that you've become a piece of me
A puzzle piece, that even out of 1,000 pieces
The only piece to be missing is "us"
And it ruins the entire puzzle
Because it isn't complete
Without one piece
The puzzle can't be finished
I'm not sure if that's better or worse
To be a mystery or to be incomplete

My Sleep Ritual

Numbers move like a pendulum
Back and forth
Right to left
10 to 1
Falling slowly
Closer together
As our eyes close
And static forms
In our vision and our ears
Static is all it takes
To fall
Fall asleep.

The British Say Tom-aww-toe

Life is so much more enjoyable
When you have a sprinkle of ambition
And your face is freckled with palpitating
Spots of desire that align randomly
Under the nebulas in your eyes

Though, without that, we are simply
Stretchy skin, bone, and liquid.

Oh . . . Poems

2020 routines piss me off
Keys, wallet, mask
Oh shit, where's my mask
4 minutes later
Got it, let's go
Suffocate in the cereal aisle
It's not hard to breathe,
Just hard to live
Over a computer
Only 17 followers would know
If something deadly happened
And that's a lot of people for
2021

Dear COVID-19, I Hate You
(Sincerely Me)

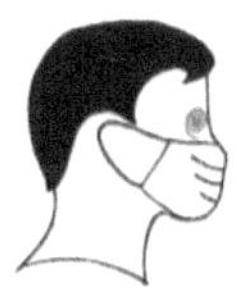

You are my cup of 2 A.M. water
You are the thing I need the most after a drunken night
You are the source of satisfaction in the drowsy mornings
You are not needed, but desperately wanted in the A.M.

You are my cup of 3 A.M. water
You taste of nothing, yet you are the flavor of life
You are the thing I yearn for when I've fallen too far
You are the only thing that can make me sober again

You are my cup of 4 A.M. water
You are only convenient when I can't see straight
You are useful like the glow of the moon and stars at night
You are only desirable when I beg for you

You are my cup of 5 A.M. water
You are to leave after I've had my fill
You are to not come back until the next sun falls
What we have is only for the A.M.

A.M. Water

Anxiety is your worst enemy
You could do everything perfect for someone; wear their favorite color, smile when you see them, hug them every chance you get. But just because you can't say "I like You," you get let down when they don't notice it. Or when they don't notice you. Your everything becomes nothing to them just because you can't say those 3 words.

The Cat Clawed My Tongue

I've got nothing to do and nothing to say
Sometimes I wish my thoughts would walk away
If I could get a sunny day to turn to grey
I might actually feel happy
Cuz I'm sick of the black and white
But the blend makes me think too much
So much that I end up crying on your floor
But you aren't able to hear it
I try to hide my tears and play it off with a watery eyed yawn.
Honestly I hate thinking so much
So much that I don't recognize my own mind
So much that I honestly just want to drink again
And I know that brings out the worst in me
And I'm being repetitive but I'm being so honest right now
And it's moments like these when I scare myself
I don't understand why I get so sad
Even though you want me to talk but I have nothing to say
I just need some space to think but
I don't want to be away from you
Which is why you don't understand why I'm upset. To you it
would be easy to manage. But you aren't in my shoes.

I'm On My Period.

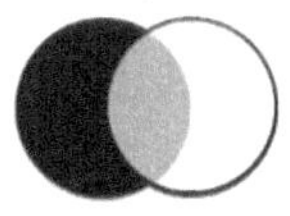

Your words are as sharp as razors
Your throat fuels my pain
If I wanted to slit my wrists
I should let you kiss my vein

Rated "R"

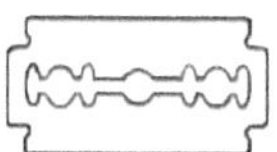

We really are so damn
Selfish
That we want what we can't have
But what we can have, wants us
Yet we don't want that
Because it isn't good enough

You're Not A Movie Star

when someone passes away, the one that actually feels dead
is the one that is still living
when speaking during a eulogy, the one that is still living
is more silent than the deceased
when attending a funeral, everyone forgets to mention that
it's not "fun" at all.

Here Are Your Damn Flowers

Your books smell different
In a distant, unsatisfying way
I expect must and
Dust
But only smell
Fresh printed ink
That resembles a laminated page
Who knew "new" would smell so
Sad

Plastic Is Pathetic

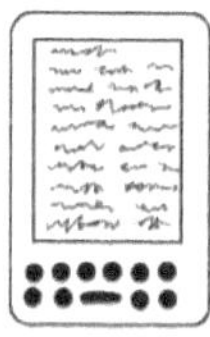

Philosophy and I are
Strange Acquaintances alike
They say that losing your mind
Is more detrimental than
Losing your body

I'm Friends with Plato

Whenever I stay there, it's like you're still here.
Your spirit floats in the air
Though I know you're nowhere near.
The music meets my ears and it reminds me of your voice.
It reminds me of the way you moved.
I look in the crowd, hoping to find your face
But the shadows deceive my eyes once again
I still wait for the day when you might come back.
I could spot you in a crowd of dark faces. I knew the shape of
your body too well

Ballet and Business Homework

Salt turns to
Sting turns to
Sand turns to
Scab turns to
Scratch turns to
Scar

I'm Always Itchy

The smell of the honey suckle makes me nauseous as it wafts
through the sliding screen door
Hearing the folks greet each other on their morning walk
sounds like a foreign language
Seeing the sun glimmer on the pond as the birds flutter to catch
their breakfast make my eyes hurt
Everything seems wrong when you're not in the perfect
company of the perfect person
Everything is wrong

Sunny Days Make Me Puke

I forgot
I need to be a shitty person to help you uphold your status. To
make it seem like you're a saint. To make it seem like you're a
better person by simply being less terrible and making me look
like I've done worse. I can be a more terrible person so you can
redeem yourself as "nice"

Boom, Roasted

Let my trucks splash through the water
Don't care if they rust tonight
Maybe they'll fly me to
That one place
My skull on the concrete
And take me to the stars
When I can float within
A space of no band aids
Just
Myself
Just me.

My Skateboard Is A Bad Swimmer

The sandman could shovel
A beach out of the sand in the corners of my eyes
Every grain represents a different hardship
And to scoop a handful of 1,000 grains
Is already too many for a lifetime
20 or 90
A handful is too much to handle, humble soul
And even 100 years doesn't, deserve that many grains of
sadness

Mr. Sandman Is A Lifeguard

You only break after the fact
But for now, you must stay as strong as stone
But even stone can be broken with the right tool

153

Chisel My Face Off

Prayers, wishes, and hopes don't coincide
If you pray for a wish, it's a joke
If you hope for a prayer, it's selfish
And wishes? They're no better than the glitter on your eyelashes

Genies Are So F*cking Rude

But can "you" understand why it's hard to imagine?
I don't have "you"
"You" don't exist, but I wish "you" did, or will soon
Even as I write this, I'm talking to a page, not a human
It's me and my thoughts
"You" don't exist, but i can't wait for the day that "you" become a
reality for me

Stranger Danger!

Gaslight let the salty tears fall from my eyes
As my cheek burns
With a smile on my face
Because that's all I've been taught
Pretend to smile and "you'll feel better"

Practice Makes Perfect
(But Not for Basketball or Soccer)

We dream of people
Who dream of people
Dreaming of them

We're All in A Threesome

Patience.
Is it a virtue or a skill?
It varies
But variables are only for math
Which I failed

Geometry is Not My Friend

You protected someone
Aren't you proud
You made sure everyone was okay
Aren't you proud
You didn't have a cruddy night
Aren't you proud
You didn't fixate on past memories
Aren't you proud
You did what you needed to do
Aren't you proud
If only you protected them *that* night
Why aren't you PROUD.

Pool Sticks Are the New Swords

You ask where I get the bruises
How could I tell you
They are from myself
I cry so much
Rub my eyes too much
They literally scab
And bruise
Pathetic

No One Punched Me
(Unfortunately)

Trigger warning

You are no one's priority
You don't exist to your priority
What
A
Shame

But really
Does it matter?

No.

Not even
Like a crack
In the
Road.

Sniffing Sidewalks

No one really knows what goes on in my head
The boy says "lol" when I'm sad
The girl doesn't reply when I want it
The other girl doesn't realize cause I don't dare tell her
The other boy won't know cause I don't dare tell him
And I'm STUCK coping on my own
Saying "it's okay, breathe"
I practice without an audience,
Swiping away every tear at 100mph
Faking a smile around the bar strangers
Listening to the song on repeat
Regretting the time after the boy fell away
Letting the corners of my eyes burn
As the bugs crawl on my arm
Gently tickling me, but who cares
They've done no harm
Soon enough, my skin will turn to dust
As the corners of my eyes crust
And dry, as rough as sand paper
But as sensitive as nerves

The "DJ" Went Missing

Do you ever remember I'm here?
Does the rumbling of the swallow in my ears
Reach yours?
Does the scratching of my jeans
Reach out?
Reaching doesn't equivalate
To touch.

Thigh Chafing

I'll be honest.
Even a person who slightly resembles you
I'm obsessed with
They have nothing to do with you
And that's.... pathetic... silly? I can't even find the right word.
I'm attached
Literally and figuratively
I miss you, Oct. 10th.

Dates Aren't Romantic
(Calendar dates, ya know?)

Let me cry
Let me fall apart
Just let me feel broken
Don't convince me I'm not
Don't persuade me it will get better
I'm okay right now, as I am
Jesus, just let me crumble
I'll feel better
Shivering

Jesus Felt Chilly

There's no such thing as writer's block
Just laziness
Zoning out
Procrastination
Hearing the rubbing of the cricket legs at night
While the mosquitoes feast on your skin
Your eyes glaze over
Like perfectly melted sugar on the donuts
Your adhd presses pause for a moment
As your foggy mind lets your thought float
Like clouds that hide the stars at night
Too bad your mind can't write
When it's sober enough to comprehend
What you write

Mosquitoes Are Vampires

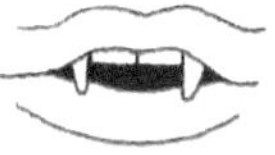

Ok but here's the thing
I will be honest with you even if you don't like it.
If they *actually* cared
They'd be waiting on the tips of their toes
For your response
Yet you're thinking on the tip of your tongue for the one
message that will get their attention

Licking Cliffs

You are nothing
Until the "you're the only one to know this"
Gets leaked at a drunken moment
You are nothing
And you're not special
But their life isn't yours
So why should it matter?
There are billions of people here
Why should you be the only one
To be told "you're the only one . . ."
It doesn't exist
And it doesn't matter
Don't take it personally

But to be that one in 7 billion
Is
Beyond incredible.
Too bad it realistically doesn't exist.

Lottery Tickets Are Fake
(Unless You're Lucky)

Drugs are an escape
As repetitive as that sounds it's true
Even alcohol (my drug, honestly)
Makes the world seem splendid
I don't know why
I don't know what chemicals are released:
There's serotonin and dopamine
But that's a stranger to exquisiteness
There's something unique
But that's the only word I can use for it

Do You Think Doing Alcohol Is Cool?

I got red stains on your white sweater
Rose tone in the cold weather
I'm sorry for all the things I've done
I really am the first to none

Sorry, High School
(Even Though I Still Despise You)

You're simply a ghost here
You hear the whispers
And they don't help
Because
They remind you of
Everything that will be
Once you're gone

No more you

But distance doesn't mean gone
And gone doesn't mean forever

This Title Doesn't Exist

N/A

Sometimes I think I really love you
But the more I think of you,
The more I forget what your face looks like
I'm in love with the idea of you
But your appearance is distorted in my memory
Because I don't look at you enough
I didn't soak up your features
If someone asked me what color eyes you had
I would have no idea what to say
Because although your eyes are focused on me in my mind
I can't recall what they look like
I'm in love with an idea
And with that logic
I could never love anyone because
A human is not an idea,
They are alive.

My Memory is Sh!t
(I'm Getting Old)

www.ingramcontent.com/pod-product-compliance
Lightning Source LLC
Chambersburg PA
CBHW030307160726
47992CB00005B/1912